Unrelated Questions

poems by Jovonna Van Pelt

artwork by Bonnie Meier Periale

Published by Human Error Publishing
Paul Richmond
www.humanerrorpublishing.com
paul@humanerrorpublishing.com

Copyright © 2019
by
Human Error Publishing & Jovonna Van Pelt
All Rights Reserved

ISBN: 978-0-9991985-8-2

"Commute, or The Greenfield to South Deerfield Rush" first appeared in *Compass Roads,* edited by Jane Yolen, Levellers Press (2018)

Human Error Publishing asks that no part of this publication be reproduced or transmitted in any form or by any means electronic or mechanical, including photocopy, recording or information storage or retrieval system without permission in writing from Jovonna Van Pelt and Human Error Publishing. We ask that you do this to support us and the artists.

*Dedicated to
Mal and Dirk
with enduring love*

Contents

those shoes   10

still life?   13

Commute   14

object lesson   15

Unrelated Questions I   17
    rollercoaster
    children
    beard
    haphazard
    definition
    lost

what is your favorite color?   20

morning mist   21

the pottery class   22

love and pottery   23

the finished pot   24

do you deserve a medal?   25

eat this much   26

Unrelated Questions II   28
    "10"
    dynamite
    late
    brochure
    city
    crow
    funnier

spiral dance   32

April   33

snapshot   34

benediction   35

breakage   37

Unrelated Questions III   40
    genius
    girls
    price
    pickle
    nonchalance
    religion
    grief

the March   44

the selkie   46

composing prophecy   48

in the moment   49

the Magic Room   51

Unrelated Questions IV   52
    lick
    Santa
    willpower
    underwear
    September
    time

a small windfall   55

we the people   56

multitasking   58

dreaming   60

stage iv in spring   61

Unrelated Questions V   62
    cuddling
    knife
    vivid
    heroes
    kerchief
    holidays

sex strike 2.0   65

thermodynamics   66

stay   67

summoning Daphne   68

swimming lessons   70

repeatable results   74

Unrelated Questions VI   75
    protection
    wine
    forgiven
    consumables
    walk
    buttress

pachyderm apocalyptic   78

Acknowledgments   81

About the Publisher   83

About the Author and Artist   84

those shoes

i.
is it worth it
just to wear those shoes?
glass slippers are less fragile than our flesh, it seems.
it will take a piece of your toe, a slice of your heel.
you give up the rest of your life and all other dreams
to wear those shoes.
whose wish is that?

ii.
he makes the offer
as though you may choose
not to wear them.
once you put on the Red Shoes,
you will never get them off.
you will keep dancing and dancing and dancing.
you
will
keep
dancing.

iii.
dancing
backwards in high heels,
Ginger
keeps
smiling.

iv.
the all-American girl
does not wear sensible shoes.
who's attracted to that?
you wear high heels
even with your bathing suit.
designed for fashion not utility,
your dainty feet are molded
for insensibility;
Ken's feet are flat.

v.
they will break your feet
to make them small
and bind them tight
in tiny shoes like jewels.
years later when revolution comes,
they will free you and
the wraps will come off.
then you will not walk at all.

vi.
in any case
you won't run away.
you can never run away.
you couldn't run to save your life.

not in those shoes.

still life?

on the worn blue table
a bowl of fruit imitates art.
Sunday noon sunlight streams
through the window,
dimples each surface ...
a drowsy hour
after you are gone.
it is warm here and the fruit gleams.
simple pleasures.
and it seems to me that
stillness
at the core of each heart
feeds our dreams:
this ripe pear,
this round apple,
the world that waits for tasting ...

Commute, or
The Greenfield to South Deerfield Rush

I drove a two-door Chevy Nova
68 miles each way:
over the Delaware, into the Poconos,
memorizing Shakespeare and show tunes on tape.
I rode the bus from Clinton NJ
to Manhattan's Port Authority
2 full hours each way:
three books a week,
plus correspondence old school, pen in hand.
now,
8 miles south from Greenfield:
under the railroad bridge,
past turnoffs for Historic Deerfield,
watchful for free-roaming chickens;
after the perennial gardens
and a vegetable stand or two;
on the right, the miracle of butterflies;
then down to the fossil shop,
I turn left
past the velociraptor
and if I'm not stuck behind
some farm tractor or a waddle of crossing ducks,
I arrive:
14 minutes door to door,
just a few CD tracks in,
or time enough to count my blessings
daily.

object lesson

driftwood stones old books
bleached bones
a bust of Nefertiti
a Mexican clay mask:
our house was built with found objects
unbound by average expectations.
jars of feathers and painted boxes
offered secret choices and
creative incantations.

i didn't imagine my mother
as a shaman
she was the minister's wife after all
but
she made magic at will
in my life.
long dead
she conjures it still.

on my altar rests
her photograph
pink baby shoes small seashells
a broken Kewpie doll
sprinkles of crushed amethyst
crystals for healing:
it all touches her touches me
revealing the mystery of objects
and mother's blood.

she taught me out loud
and by example
balance is far different
than symmetry.
not two but three, not four but five
make it bigger make a statement
be alive to the beauty of the odd thing.
this object lesson
choose the odd thing
found or bought
caught kept remade
deconstructed
or redeemed.

on my north windowsill
black pebbles from her garden
invoke Earth
long dead
she gives her bones back.
the odd things she loved are here
with me.

Unrelated Questions I

do you keep your eyes open
when you're on the rollercoaster?
the screams seem louder if they're closed,
and the plummet down more terrifying.
i'd rather see the ground coming.

could it be true that
cobblers' children have no shoes?
might it also mean
the doctor's children are hypochondriacs
and psychiatrists' kids are pathological?
i think that we can all agree where that leaves me,
the minister's eldest daughter.

could i talk you into growing a beard?
it would be softer, i think,
than your 30 grit chin
and my skin might stay on days after.
though you always burnish me
to a pretty blush pink
before i start to peel.

how will you know
when you're losing your mind?
Mom said we would probably find her shoes
in the refrigerator.
that hasn't happened, but
so many things are
fairly haphazard now.

what is your definition
of "sexually experienced"?
would it be 20 years
with one sweetly curious lover
or 20 chance encounters in serial monogamy?
asking for a friend.

of course.

---

what have you lost?
glasses are on your head,
phone appears to be in your pocket,
and car keys are in your hand.
i can identify the empirical stuff.
the meaning of your life is up to you.

what is your favorite color?

at this current size
i wear my share of black,
but red is my favorite.
red is a statement.
it was once the only color for lipstick.
it matches everything.
red is a balloon, a clown nose.
red is the wagon i pulled my baby brother in.
red rover, red rover, he crosses over.
red is messy life, messy death,
a bloody rag or raging war that does not end.
in some places red is the bride.
love indeed is a red red rose;
all other roses are something else.
red is the opposite of nonchalant.
red is committed and loud.
it is not shy.
red shoes for dancing,
red sky at morning.
red is my color.

morning mist

i never leave
the water's edge
empty-handed.
in younger days,
it often meant
a pocket
full of angry poems.
but this morning…
o, this morning
i gather peace
like water forms mist.

on the other side
of this fog-kissed pond
who knows?
it might be Avalon.

the pottery class

i feel the disapproval
long before his actual words
not unkind but firm
we're forming a cylinder
he reminds me
tall and narrow
pulled up slowly from the base
evenly proportioned
he repeats the motions
and instructions
tall and narrow.
he points
i scan the rest of the class
busily cooperating
each making their proto-vase
totally tubular.
clay-spattered dripping slurry
i look down at the raw wet bowl
spinning in front of me
apparently
despite good intentions
i only go fast and deep and wide
i say honestly
i think you're messing
with primal forces of nature here.

love and pottery

he tells us
either you go pro eventually
or you stop making pottery.
perhaps
he thinks this work isn't art or
you run out of people to give it to.
his craft is so professional
no human hand is visible
in his plates and cups.
but that's where he's wrong–
friends will always accept
the beautiful bowl with the wobbled edge
from your flawed hand and your perfect heart.

the finished pot

surprising myself
i throw a perfect pot
the shape of harmonious creation
generous mouth open
walls of tensile strength and even thickness
round belly smooth skin ample foot
before the firing
i incise the bottom with a spiral
homage to the goddess
and decorate the lip with simple lines
a hieroglyph of awe and thanks.
the finished pot sings
and so
i give it to my mother
whose beauty is also earth and water
air and fire.

do you deserve a medal?

my friend Linda
thinks she should have a medal
for all the things she doesn't say
when provoked. that's probably right,
knowing her vocabulary.
my neighbor wants a prize
for massaging kale by the bushel.
i think that i took one for the team
in the summer of nineteen-seventy,
when i taught French kissing to all the boys
who needed it.
i imagine my legacy
of happy lovers and wives,
but there's no way to track
the lives i've touched
with lips & teeth & tongue.

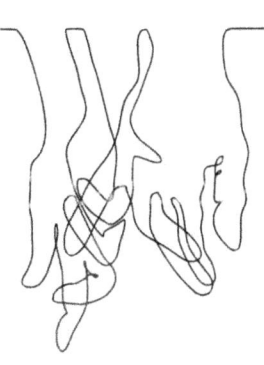

eat this much

the side of his fork cuts through
pale limply steamed brussel sprouts on my plate—
or slices of cold pickled beets
or piled lima beans—
neatly dividing them
into precisely equal clumps.
the tines of his fork
tap tap tap
pointing out the new half portion.
this is good for you he says
you must eat this much.
i do not.

Mom makes hamburger 101 ways
our mainstay version all consumed
the serving dish is cleared
my glass of milk is empty
the family is waiting
so am i.
the fork descends
half portion cut in two
Tap Tap Tap
Just Eat This Much.
i do not touch it.

glistening orange gelatin
jiggles on the table
ready for a dab of canned whipped cream
no dessert until we finish.
i am waiting.
my father's fork hovers again
he cleaves the quarter portion down
to one small mouthful
pushes it scratching sideways
forming a simple square.
Tap. Tap. Tap.
Eat. This. Much.
all the air has been sucked out of our kitchen
in the silence.
i breathe first
then swallow it down
the family devours their jello.
i steal a subversive glance
at brother's secret smile.

we discovered early on
i can eat
a single bite
of anything.

Unrelated Questions II

who among us is a "10" for long?
my own title claim to Sex Goddess of the World
was brief.
what a relief to have other skills
and a day job.

did she tell you
her parents taught themselves how to use dynamite?
they were good at it.
blowing things up is easy.
saving them is harder.

isn't 60 kind of late to start?
yes, for some things:
ballerina, astronaut,
the world's youngest violin prodigy.
no, for others.
late blooming is better than not,
plus we value artisanal so much more now.

do you have a brochure for that?
no, Dad, it isn't a congregational church.
it's a pagan circle:
we're tree-huggers, witches, nudists, and herbalists,
existential humanists who practice magic
and sacrifice virgins.
oh, that's nice, dear. pass the salt.

what did i learn today?
our town is actually a city,
not by population but form of government.
this seems important:
we choose it for ourselves
and size doesn't matter.
at least in this case.

have you ever seen a crow
leaving bread to feed a field mouse?
i marvel at such sacred gifts.
i remember to light a candle and
send a larger check to my local food pantry.

don't we get funnier as we get older?
i hope that's true.
i'm laughing over us
all the time
and i'd hate to think it's just me.

spiral dance

into the green mountain
down to the grounding place
i
      go
            down
to meet you in the ritual space
where a single candle burns
in a cave full of light
we open arms and begin
our bright shadows dance together
your hair like skeins of night
as we spin
the incense smokes to scented ash
and more join in
as all our feet take magic flight
in the spiral dance
at the heart of the mountain.

when i awake again
i still hear your footfall
sacred dancer
in the hall of dreams.

April

April comes to us.
spring's delicate days
hold us
like fledgling birds.
when will we fly?
it takes time to grow wings.
patience.
breathe slowly.
the sun must warm us awhile.

snapshot

in this one
the parsonage yard is green
shrubs in early bloom
it must be Easter
and we are in our Sunday review finery
brother still in short pants
sister wearing disgruntled curls
me in patent leather shoes
and Mom
tall, taut, mysterious,
in sadness i can only imagine.

benediction

i could say
on the day Leonard Cohen died
i got drunk,
made love like a demon,
spent time in a hazy funk of old jazz
and city skyline, smooth skin
and half-tried Bible verses,
turning wine into words again.

actually
i found out the day after.
he might like
the tribute-in-hindsight,
even from my unblessed lips,
but he would call me out
for lying.
truth was Eliezer's song.

when i believed life would be beautiful,
his was the music
of rags and midnight.
beauty has its own
brief prayers, fearful sacrifice, sudden blessings.
would he recognize
this tenuous mix of faith and flesh,
the flux of soul and self?

the psalm of praise, the upheld knife,
the tearful rituals of life and hope?
and now
all earthly rites are done.
the only words remaining
both thanks and benediction:
go in peace.

breakage

in our front hall
Abraham Lincoln's bust
sat
on a tall white stand:
my mother's sainted hero,
a thrift shop find, already
chinks in the casting
that she plastered and painted.
but
nothing survived in our house for long.
we knocked Abe over so many times
that gluing his head back on
became her dogged ritual
until
the missing chips around his throat
made an irreparable wound.
so much breakage.

breakage:
in the trade
it is the expected amount,
compensation calculated
for what is damaged or lost
in transit.

it comes down
to percentage or cost.
losses are anticipated
and
it does not matter
where the wreckage lies.

it does not matter
where the wreckage lies
or
who picks up.
salvage what you can.
try the super glue, duct tape, zip ties.
try the book club, therapy, brew pub, meditation,
yoga, internet, hive mind.
the broken bits cannot be fixed
or
left behind,
and all the scars still show.

all the scars still show
outside and in:
the damaged skin, the cautious thought,
lost time, the terrible choices.
so many days alone.
who was that

on the phone you did not answer?
sometimes
you cannot bear the sound
of other voices.
words don't always help, even when
the silence is broken.

when the silence is broken
there may be
too much truth told.
we think we can be strong or free.
we think we will be whole
because
human flesh heals over.

flesh heals over
but
it is never new again.
so much breakage.

Unrelated Questions III

> what is the half-life of genius?
> Madame Curie's journal is still radioactive.
> a lead-lined archival box
> keeps us from knowing it.

> what are little girls made of?
> whatever.
> we can probably grow out of it.
> i am not your sugar.
> i am not your spice.
> i am often not sweet and sometimes not nice.
> in the end, i am okay with that.

do you know what it is to be female?
there is a price:
though all the time it feels like knives,
you give up your voice and your mermaid's tail
to walk on feet, to watch love fail.

---

what precisely is your plan
for that half-jar of pickle juice?
you ate the last pickle some time ago,
yet carefully reserved the empty brine
in the fridge.
i await with bated breath
a culinary delight of dilled perfection
and hell freezing over.

wasn't it Whitman who coined the phrase
"perfect nonchalance"?
amazing.
he never saw you sitting naked
centered in a king-size bed
propped by a legion of pillows
laptop on your knees and
reading glasses down your nose,
relaxed and sovereign.
lord of all.

oh my.

---

should we study Religion or practice it?
the answer could come down to
a personal need for Proof
versus a wish for Faith.
forced to choose all my life,
i took Art and Love instead.

why didn't someone tell me?
i didn't know about grief.
there isn't some other side
you come out
once you've moved through the stages.
grief moves with you.

the March

we Mobilized for Women's Lives
November 1989
two busloads from New Jersey N.O.W.
in suffragette white
came with me to the Pentagon's lot—
in this country
the lords of war have more than enough parking.
a million of us regrouped on the Mall
looped the White House chanting CHOICE
i worked the shifting fringe of the crowd
selling buttons to pay for the buses.
it was somewhere on First Street
she waved me over
an old woman
leaning one-handed on her walker
starting to tip
i steadied her she nodded thanks
a tear spilled into the creases of her cheek
i want to buy a button she said
i lost my sister to a bloody butcher
she was seventeen
70 years and not a day that i don't miss her
70 years and i am still angry about her death
on her white cardigan sweater
i pinned our button like a Purple Heart.
she said i wish i were marching with you
i touched my own wet cheek to hers
you are, sister, you are.

the March surged on around her
fierce and frail she stood her ground
i lost sight
as the crowd moved on
but she came home with me that day.
i think of her
i don't give up the fight
our arms are tired from carrying these signs
our bones ache from long miles marching
but these bodies are ours, we get to choose
our voices are strong and we speak together
not one more sister
not one more daughter niece neighbor friend
not one more woman.

not one more.

the selkie

there was nothing extraordinary
about her childhood
she did not stand out
among the other swimmers
truant beachcombers
weathered bones cracked shells tumbled stones
also abandoned at the tide line.
at nineteen she left the shore
married a man drawn to ministry as his mask
she bore two daughters and a son.
parish halls filled and emptied
like tidal pools of judgment
the surge and clash
of Sunday tea and expectations
beat her womanskin smooth.
she buried secrets in impenetrable depths
collected driftwood broken vows souvenirs
of oceans lost

trapped in an airless parsonage
she died
missing the wind and salt spray.
  would you recognize a selkie if you saw one?
  how would we know her
  after she was lured from the sea
  for a life on land?
  even her own children might think her ordinary
  among the altar flowers and stained glass.
her sealskin was never found.

at my open window
in her honor
a jar of seashells warmed by sun
and under my bed
shoes full of sand.

composing prophecy

foretell the way the end is coming
begin with time of day
remember to mention
how everything smells
like grass or toast or rain
give us a clue
when it's coming and how
use onomatopoeia
remember to include sounds
of waves or thunder or birdsong
just in case it's pleasant to linger on
in the last moments
remember to tell me
who else is there
and if we've been happy.

in the moment

while you looked away for a moment
i took a fortifying deep breath
adjusted the chair pillow
reached again for my coffee
smiling just in time to meet your eyes
in my head
Winona Ryder says
"take me away from all this death."

when i was a witch
in that healing circle of wymmin
casting their hopes as spells
within the Wheel That Turns
death seemed unlikely.
we could join hands
we could open our arms
so wide
life would always last long enough
when i was a witch
wishes had magic
belief was young and easy.

grief is harder
than anyone confesses
not least of all because it is
mathematical, exponential
zero is a theory that experience disproves
there is never nothing
we all start with something
one small grief that adds, that multiplies
that piles on like a doubling curse
we become the walking wounded
the metaphoric undead
maybe that explains zombies, vampires,
monsters under the bed
grief posits a problem
fear proves
nothing does exist
zero is
we are alone after all.

fear
is in the eyes you turn back to me
but i have made a rational decision
in the moment of breath
while you are still here
there is no death
no grief
no zero
there is all the love we need.

the Magic Room

what used to be enhancement
segued into damage control
or even—perish the thought—crisis management.
the dash of lip gloss
the flick of mascara
the spritz of perfume
is now fifteen minutes of planned reconstruction
daily.

i remember
when the results of the Magic Room
were insufficient to satisfy her,
my mother renamed it the Miracle Room
and spent more time there.
we all laughed.

but who's laughing now?
i gaze blearily at my mirror
into her aging face each morning
and wonder
how much work this will take or
how much longer i need to do it.

Unrelated Questions IV

why not lick every last crumb from this plate?
say exactly what you mean.
there is no need now
to worry about what other people think.
do not settle. do not repent.
keep everything that is meaningful
right until the end.
even before you are gone we will forgive you.

how old were you when
you stopped believing in Santa Claus?
i was 8 catching my parents smuggling toys downstairs.
for siblings' sakes i kept quiet.
funny about that
i've believed again for a long time now.

who says i don't have willpower?
even as we speak i am not eating
the New York-style cheesecake
marbled with rich chocolate fudge and
topped with luscious red raspberry sauce
that flung itself importunate
into my shopping cart last night.

i deserve a treat.

and how are you fixed for socks and underwear?
Mom used to say it all the time
and Grammy too.
maybe it's a woman's thing
when you're getting too close.
it means ask me something else.
it means you've asked too much.

do you actually celebrate New Year's?
January doesn't feel like a real fresh start.
even at this advancing age, i prefer
September and new school supplies.
the year begins again
with a fresh pencil and blank notebook.
i can't wait to find out
what we're learning next.

can't we get more time?
i didn't think much about the ticking clock
until it was a ticking bomb on a runaway train
under an avalanche during an earthquake
triggered by the approaching meteor.
i'm gonna need a few more minutes.

a small windfall

the US postal service is currently
handling my order of a t-shirt
that will say to the world
"I'm an American and I'm so sorry."
most of us are very sorry.
it may be necessary
to wear the shirt to rags
then reorder–
2020 seems far far away.
in the interim
the balance of my small windfall
has been split between a needy friend
families separated at our border
and a Planned Parenthood donation
for Mike Pence's birthday.
a little found money
is a wonderful thing.

we the people

we are not for sale
you cannot own us
our wombs are not subject to
your prurient old white men's fingers
and secret fantasies
you are not the masters
we are not the slaves
our work is not for sale
at 30%, 40%, 50% less
because we are not white men
our health is not for sale
to your corporate hospitals and insurance magnates
our air and rivers and mountains are not for sale
to your chemical polluters and your strip mining
your voracious industrial greed and
your self-absorbed billionaire acquisitions
we cannot be bought with lies
we cannot be silenced with lies
even your lies aren't loud enough
we cannot be bought
by your smug collusion and hypocrisy
we are not complicit
in your wastefulness
your disdain
your casual violence
we are not for sale
we cannot be bought or silenced
you will have to keep killing us

women's bodies matter to us
black lives matter to us
all families' lives, healthy lives
life, liberty, and the pursuit of happiness
actually matter for all of us
we know that does not matter to you
we are done asking
now we are telling you
we are not for sale
now we are demanding
women's bodies matter
black lives matter
parents and children matter
clean air and clean water matter
stop lying to us
clean government matters
stop lying to us and do your jobs
stop trying to buy us
with fake sincerity and tax cuts
that never trickle down
we are not for sale
we cannot be silenced
we demand real government
we demand respect
we the people
we are the people
and we are not for sale.

multitasking

at this very moment
i'm losing an argument
with the universe
about how much fun blondes actually have.

at this very moment
i am outliving Grampa
who died at 61 from
emphysema and disappointment.
he could play the ukele
and always sang my name
to the tune of "Ramona."

at this very moment
i am actively engaged
in the benevolent neglect of my garden.
flora that survive will foster
the next biological wave and possibly
insect rule of the planet.

at this very moment
i must tell you
i never intend to be obscure.
i want words to resonate
upon first hearing
i want to say them out loud.
we women know that silence
is not our friend.

at this very moment
i am not forgiving my father
for saying he never wanted me.

like a death camp guard hiding in Argentina,
he is old sick caught
almost pitiful
it doesn't make him less guilty.
he wasted little time on me.
i do not forget.

at this very moment
days are slipping over the edge
when we first learned the meaning of
glioblastoma
we were measuring in months.
we are losing our friend
she is not losing us.

at this very moment
my benevolent neglect also extends to
the cleanliness of my car
paid invoice filing
and the birthdays of cousins once-removed.
it's no longer tolerable for citizenship;
still twitching from last night's news
i am marching again.

at this very moment
there is little reason to expect that
Justin Trudeau is sending the limo
to pick me up
though one should not lose all hope.
that way lies madness.
madness as it turns out
runs in the family
but insanity
and male-pattern baldness
stop here.

dreaming

to dream of things isn't wrong, is it?

it's one way to tell the future ...the past we summon with seances or photographs ... the present we work with ordered lives of schedules and short-term expectations ... but the future ... ah, the future is not so sure ... in our hands we clutch the actuarial charts, tarot cards, Quequeg's thrown bones, a Magic Eight Ball ... minds speculate on the unknown possibilities, dreams populate our nightscape with desires and the deeds of imagination.

as a girl i remember dreaming so vividly i felt the physical pangs of grief when my daytime closet held no sparkling ballgowns ... the midnight mind-wandering Hollywood-hash musicals never produced a hit song or a permanent dance partner ... such dreams were not predictions, the life that followed hardly wish fulfillment.

then how to deal with the present reality of life more full of memory than promise? unless i'm living to 120, i have done with middle age altogether, careening toward my dotage without a plan of the future or any practical sense.

to dream of things, tiaras and top hats ... to conjure patience and plenty ... to hope for a future story ... it is not wrong to dream of things ...

but be wary when you read the bones.

stage iv in spring

the world is not quite green
but soon.
longer days are almost warm enough;
spring comes,
equal measures of light and dark.
we are not dying yet.
March breezes that fret and freshen
move air through those lungs.
both feet press against the thawing earth.
he is still here. what more to hope for?
count the days but not their number.
there is time enough, we say,
but do not waste a minute
now.
let the gentler green peek through.
he holds his children soft
as buds on branches and smiles at me,
pretending to make summer plans.
set some grief aside awhile.
we are not dying yet.

Unrelated Questions V

will you read my book?
if i call it "skin hunger"
therapists among you might advise i pay
for professional cuddling
and save my breath.
not to mention all the ink and trees.

is that knife sharp?
whatever you're cutting
the last thing you want
is a dull blade
or a hack job.

how to describe you?
vivid
is meant for colors or light,
bright and strong—
the wings of rare birds, stars and the blood moon—
impossible to forget.
you are so vivid
i conjure you
with the simplest of summonings:
closed eyes and a deep breath.

how can you think
there are no more heroes?
you rescue me.
every day.

shall we talk about pain?
my mother shaved off all her hair once
instead of suicide.
stubble marked her mute rebellion.
a red kerchief was the badge of her despair.

how will i survive?
it's another round of holidays
with insular relatives and
jellied cranberry sauce from cans.
at least with crushed whole berries,
credible links to the natural world seem possible.

sex strike 2.0

> *On March 25, 2019, NASA cancelled the first*
> *all-women's spacewalk because there was only*
> *one medium-sized spacesuit.*

i have loved my share of geeks—
probably more than my share, truth be told
because smart is always sexy—
but i've had it now
i'm quitting.
those uncommunicative, math-worshipping,
pocket-protecting, screen-addicted,
socially awkward, idiot-savant quantum theorists—
those thoughtless and ungrateful men—
launched our sisters
into the black and airless void
with one spacesuit that fit.
one.
are you kidding me?!
ohhh, this is one betrayal too much
of basic human decency.
i'm done
i'm swearing off rocket scientists
and all the others too.
Lysistrata had the right idea, girls—who's with me?
in our digital electronic age
we can do it even better.
i just need to buy some batteries first.

thermodynamics

earth warms.
dry ground hardens and cracks.
blue ice whitens, calves.
salt sea seeps through barriers built by civilization.
has an apocalyptic reclamation begun?
our ocean planet bubbles and stirs.

flames finger the split kindling and flick skyward.
under a cross-hatched quilt of stars,
torches dot the darkness like lightning bugs in summer dusk.
we gaze upward.
you wrap an arm around me like a heavy cloak.

heat rises.
temperatures climb.
when we are skin to skin,
we cannot help but add to the warming.
we become one ember … then one ash.

ice becomes living water becomes clouds
becomes rain becomes green trees
becomes tinder becomes flame
becomes heat becomes passion
then motion, then stillness,
warming, rising.

no energy
generated in our universe
is lost.

stay

when the time comes
like my ancient cat
i may ask that
you stroke my head
kiss my wizened face
whisper how i am your favorite
    truth or not
tell me you will always love me
and stay
stay right here
until they close my eyes.

summoning Daphne

steady traffic on Route 2 threatens her stillness.
stillness
among the trees
is a matter of quiet
and breath.
she wonders, fingering
the raw bark edge of the bowl,
what sculptor described his art as chipping away
unnecessary pieces?
worked and waxed though it is by human hands,
essence remains
linking this wood to mythic trees.
she turns her face
and closes eyes against the sun,
summoning Daphne.
leaves sprout in her hair.
toes grow into the dark earth.
bark spreads
over hand then arm, across her breast.
it reaches her mouth as she sighs
and the highway noise intrudes.
she opens her eyes,
cradling the bowl,
still standing at the roadside array
where weathered boards
display the carver's necessary pieces.

home now
she blesses the bowl with fruit
scattered acorns
pressed leaves.
she brings the sacred outside
in,
a seasonal ritual.
no need to sacrifice a virgin.

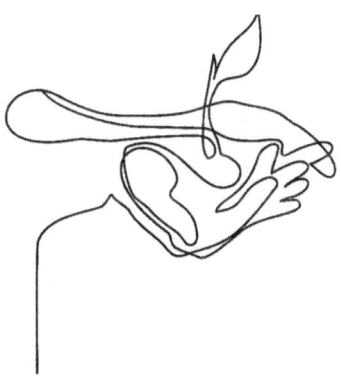

swimming lessons

in the next room
voices pressured the walls
with expanding intensity
even at low volume
the timber frame surged
with tirades, tears
breath-holding silence.
they fought
longer than she could listen
she drifted asleep
to the crashing ebb and flow
dreaming of water too rough
for swimming.

she was an excellent swimmer
like all of the family women.
hadn't her aunt challenged the Channel
in rubber cap and Black Magic bathing suit
slathered in grease to avoid hypothermia
or close human contact,
hailed the hometown heroine until
death by recliner and agoraphobia?
hadn't her mother dived into life
as a minister's wife headfirst
after eight quick weeks of courtship
and one baby-making date rape?

hadn't she the baby herself
been repeatedly pushed into the deep end?
lucky to be buoyant
to sleep through the sinking sounds
and the unanswered prayers.

a hallway light stayed on all night
to keep monsters away.
in his church study
or basement tidal cave
radio broadcasts drowned out the noise
of all family life above.
he surfaced every Sunday
smiling
fingering a Bible
shaking hands as though capable of loving.
his wife knew better
after he'd torn out her mermaid tongue.

a large mirror reflected
her coming-of-age
one bedroom wall matte black
for artistic effect
poems in white chalk
pooled around pictures of lakes
posters of ocean beaches past reach
in the dark swell of the dreaming wall
only one window
it did not open.
going downstairs was inevitable.

her mother moved the furniture
again, as if
a new floor plan was escape
to someplace different.
even sanctuary
is not the same as rescue—
temporary
like treading water
until arms and legs go numb
and body sinks.

it wasn't calm enough to float
dark closed in over her head
she rocketed up and out again
the water was never still
the sun never warmed it
bobbing up and down gulping air
she couldn't protect herself
from undertows that dragged her in
spit her out
spluttering cold confused
she just got used to the currents
and the changing temperatures.

she swam short laps
the backstroke the scissor kick
she wrapped both arms around
to hold on
slippery when wet.

what a person can get used to
life underwater
how long can she hold her breath?

repeatable results

did you know that *Frankenstein*
was published in 1818? two hundred years,
but Mary Shelley could have written it
yesterday.
we conceive then create
the creature
and robot AI,
the bomb, thalidomide,
Frankenfood,
ghettos, AR-15s, real monsters.
we do not learn.
we shift responsibility.
we flee the scene.
the "quality of mercy" escapes us.

we never quantify compassion
as the best repeatable result.

Unrelated Questions VI

did you bring a condom?
you've got binoculars in your backpack,
but no protection.
i guess we're just making out then,
or bird-watching.
take your pick.

is that wine in your travel mug, Dad?
yes, it's probably pinot grigio.
that's illegal, even in Connecticut—
you cannot drink while driving.
don't worry, he says between sips,
i'm not going very far.

what else can i do?
i forgave my little brother
long ago
for losing all my Barbie shoes.
i've forgiven him
for regularly beating me at Scrabble
and even for thinking that i'm not funny.
aggressive lung cancer will kill him soon.
how can i forgive him that?

---

why are you dragging all those things around?
photos, old books, boxes of long-playing records …
you'll never be free
if you need a moving van before you can run.
pack light, buy consumables.
"leave the gun, take the cannoli."
the path to unencumbered happiness can be yours.

what did you find today?
on my early morning walk, i found a key
to unknown treasure,
five dollars
for a deluxe bagel with coffee,
and
the edge of the sunlit world.

---

don't you appreciate a good flying buttress?
part graceful architecture,
part structural brace.
each of us could probably use
a little heavy load displacement.
(now what to do about the weight of the world …)

pachyderm apocalyptic

at the end of the world
I will be wearing
a feather boa
of bright flamingo pink
and
riding an elephant, I think,
into the star burst
of our extinction event.
those style choices will be easy;
it's living well until then.
today is harder
than tomorrow,
I swear.

tomorrow, I swear,
I will do more.
dishes will be washed, bills paid.
I will be productive, thoughtful, kind.
I will find the time
to get everything done,
each item on the list and then some.
reverie is a total distraction,
an iota of indecision a waste.
do more, think less.
there isn't much time.

there isn't much time.
what choices will you make?
kiss on the first date.
don't wait, like the good girls.
exploit every mistletoe opportunity.
better the well-rumpled bed,
the sharpened brain, the full heart.
better the unrepentant community
of lovers
than these fearful saints.
the roar of defiance
should drown out the prayers.
leave dishes in the sink.
regrets will be useless
when the time comes.

the time comes,
regardless of your planning.
pack the bug-out bag
with cheap shiny beads
or Treasury bonds—
it makes no difference.
damn the torpedoes.
stay with me tonight.
the elephant is patiently parked
outside.

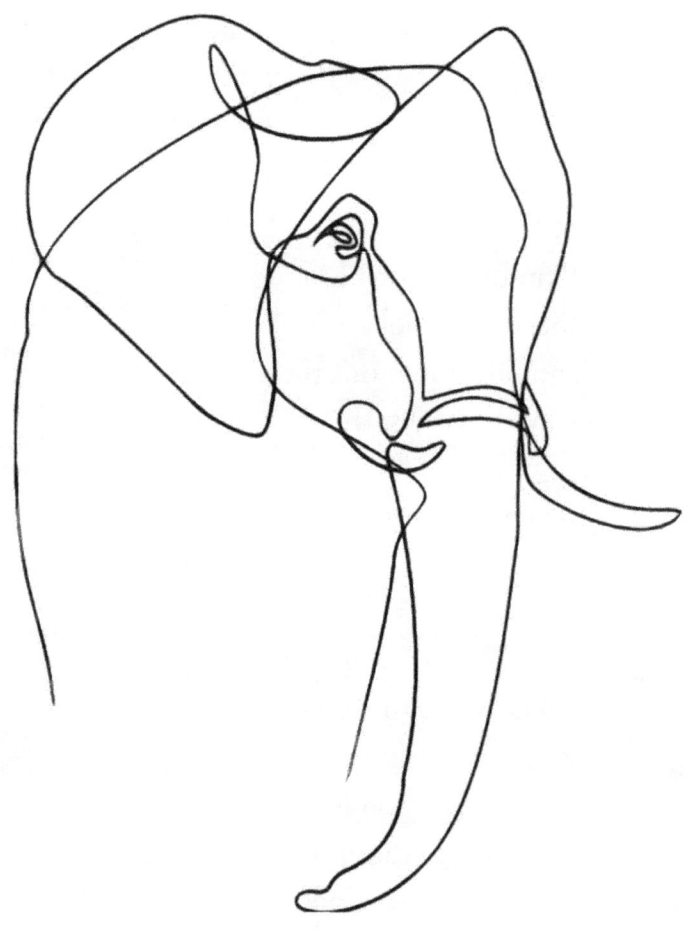

Acknowledgments

Thank you, Bonnie Meier Periale, artist, illustrator, graphic designer, sounding board, friend, goddess. You amaze me.

My heartfelt thanks to the good friends who served as peer reviewers and editors: Andrew Periale, Karen Larsen, Diane Griffin, Carla Cooke, Laura Phelps, Terrie Ilaria. I could not have managed this process without you.

Thank you to Paul Richmond of Human Error Publishing who made this book—and so many others—possible. Your enthusiasm for the written and spoken word is life-sustaining.

I am indebted to the loved ones who inspired, prodded, and aided me along this path—you have all been essential. My endless appreciation goes out to the sisters of my writing circle who shared the adventure week after week. Thanks to the many friends and members of Straw Dog Writers Guild of Western Massachusetts who made encouraging noise whenever I used you as a captive audience. This Valley is a writer's dream.

Human Error Publishing is an independent publishing company dedicated to indie artists of all types. Under the direction of Paul Richmond, HEP sponsors performances, weekly radio show, and monthly readings; annual events like the North Quabbin Garlic & Arts Festival Word Stage in Orange, MA, and the Great Falls Spoken Word Festival in Turners Falls, MA; and more.

Go to www.humanerrorpublishing.com.

About ...

Jovonna Van Pelt edited her high school newspaper and wrote English class assignments in rhymed couplets of iambic pentameter for fun. She considered a degree and career in journalism but was advised that she wasn't tough enough; it may even have been true. Through the years, her writing has served colleagues and performing artists, corporations and puppet companies. Eventually, she found a home in the Pioneer Valley of western Massachusetts and started writing for herself. Jo has been a finalist in the Poet's Seat competition, a frequent contributor to poetry open mics and spoken word fests, a member of the Straw Dog Writers Guild and a selected poet in their recent anthology *Compass Roads*, edited by Jane Yolen. This is her first published volume of poetry.

Bonnie Meier Periale may be better known as co-director of the Emmy-nominated Perry Alley Theatre, performing at the Smithsonian Institution, The Center for Puppetry Arts (Atlanta) and theaters across the USA and overseas; but she has been a graphic designer, painter and photographer throughout her life. She has been the designer of PUPPETRY INTERNATIONAL magazine for 30 years (receiving the George Latshaw Award). She and her husband-partner-in-puppetry designed the Velcro Puppet Playhouse line of toys (Parent's Choice Award). Bonnie has had several one-woman shows of her artwork and lately has been drawn to the simple art of sketching.

www.ingramcontent.com/pod-product-compliance
Lightning Source LLC
Chambersburg PA
CBHW031208090426
42736CB00009B/832